Nicole Ondatje

Not Today, Butterflies!
A Book About Food Allergy Anxiety

Bumblebee Books
London

A CIP catalogue record for this title is
available from the British Library.

ISBN: 978-1-83934-015-4

Bumblebee Books is an imprint of
Olympia Publishers.

First Published in 2021

Bumblebee Books
Tallis House
2 Tallis Street
London
EC4Y 0AB

Printed in Great Britain

www.olympiapublishers.com

Dedication

For Evynne, the bravest kid I know.

This is Quinn. Quinn is nine years old. She loves to read books, play soccer, and pretend she is a veterinarian.

She is also allergic to peanuts, meaning she can get very sick if she eats them.

This week is a big week for Quinn, she has her annual allergy doctor appointment, an afterschool playdate with Emma, and Emma's big birthday bash.

After school on Monday, Quinn's mom is going to take her to see the allergy doctor for her annual allergy exam.

That means she will have to get her blood drawn and do a skin prick test to check for other food allergies.

Quinn doesn't like going to the doctor, especially the allergy doctor.

During story hour on Monday, Quinn can hardly pay attention. All she can think about is the dreaded hour that her mom picks her up from school.

"Be brave, Quinn! Like that time you walked across the monkey bars in front of the whole class," she tells herself.

But when 3pm comes, Quinn gets the jitters; her heart races, her hands get sweaty, and her stomach feels yucky like it has rocks tumbling around in it. Her mom calls those tumbling rocks the 'worry butterflies'.

Mom remembers to bring Professor Squiggles in the car. Quinn snuggles him tight while Mom reminds her about the mindful breathing they've been practicing to help Quinn calm herself.

"Close your eyes and place your hands on your belly. Breathe in so deeply that your belly rises. Pay attention to how the air coming in your nose feels as you count to three. Then blow the air out of your mouth to a count of three and feel your belly fall," Mom says.

Quinn tries mindful belly breathing for a few minutes. Then she practices a couple of snake breaths, making a long 'ssssssssssssssssss' sound each time she breathes out.

She is definitely feeling calmer, and the worry butterflies are taking a break from flying around.

But when they pull into the parking lot, Quinn starts to panic again. By the time Nurse Penny calls Quinn and leads them back to the doctor's office, Quinn thinks she might throw up the butterflies.

During the skin prick test, Quinn cries and squirms so much that Mom needs to bear-hug her to keep her still.

Nurse Penny asks Quinn if she can close her eyes, take some deep breaths, and imagine that she is in a happy place, like at the beach playing in the sand or floating on a cloud over a rainbow.

"NO!" Quinn hollers. In the end, Nurse Penny calls the doctor to hold Quinn's arms and legs still while they take her blood sample.

Afterwards, Mom hugs Quinn as they take some deep breaths together to calm down. Mom asks Quinn if the tests really hurt or if they were just scary.

Quinn says, "It only pinched a little, but it was scary. The worry butterflies were going crazy!"

On Thursday after school, Quinn has a play date at the park with Emma. They have so much fun pretending to be pirates sailing through stormy waters to find treasure.

Emma's mom brought cookies from Sally's Bakery, and Emma offers one to Quinn. Quinn knows she can't eat cookies from a bakery, even if they are not the peanut butter kind, because some bakeries use peanuts in their kitchen. But it's hard for Quinn to speak up about her allergy and explain to her friends why she can't eat the same treats they are eating.

She feels the butterflies fluttering in her belly again and the burn of tears brewing in her eyes.

"No thanks," Quinn says, "my tummy hurts and I need to go home and take a rest." Emma looks sad as Quinn and her dad wave goodbye.

On the way home, Quinn hugs Professor Squiggles and tells herself that next time she will try counting slowly to ten, take a deep breath, and simply say, "No thank you, I have a peanut allergy."

On Saturday, Quinn is so excited for Emma's birthday party at Jumping Jeronimo's that she wakes up early.

As she puts on her purple party dress, she realizes she is also a little nervous. "Not today, butterflies!" she tells the worry butterflies in her belly.

On the way to the party, Mom puts on some quiet calming music, and Quinn sits in the back seat with her hands on her belly and her eyes closed.

After ten deep belly breaths, Quinn goes through the list in her head. "EpiPen in my bag? Check. Cupcake made by Mom? Check. Wet wipes for hands? Check. Emma's birthday gift? Check." She also asks Mom to be sure to read the labels on the snacks at the party.

"Of course," Mom agrees.

Jumping Jeronimo's is even bigger and more amazing than Quinn had imagined. Quinn and her friends have a contest to see who can jump the highest.

When it's time for birthday cake, Quinn can feel her heart start to beat a little faster and her hands get sweaty again. "You can do this!" she tells herself.

HAPPY 9th BIRTHDAY

Emma's dad offers Quinn a plate with cake covered in white frosting while Emma watches with anticipation. Quinn turns around, takes a giant breath into her belly, imagines saying the right words, and pictures her friends being understanding.

She turns back around and says, "No thank you, I have a peanut allergy."

Emma's dad says, "I forgot! Thanks for reminding me."

HAPPY 9th BIRTHDAY

Emma looks worried, "So you don't get to have any cake?"

Quinn opens her bag and pulls out a peanut-free chocolate cupcake that her mom made and says, "I always bring safe treats to parties, see?"

"Phew!" said Emma, and they both giggle as they bite into their delicious treats.

Before they get in the car, Mom hugs Quinn and says, "You did great today, how do you feel?"

"Magnificent!" Quinn says with a proud grin, "I told the worry butterflies to take a rest and they did!"

Note to Parents and Caregivers

Potential Causes of Food Allergy-Related Anxiety in Children
- Skin prick tests
- Blood draws
- Food challenges
- Accidental exposures and having an allergic reaction
- Using the epinephrine auto-injector
- Trying a new food
- Going to new environments
- Being different from friends
- Having to speak up about food allergies

Possible Signs of Anxiety

- Physical Signs: shaking, crying, stiffening body, or complaining of ailments like headaches, stomachaches, or other pain.
- Behavioral Signs: being uncooperative, argumentative, irritable, aggressive, or withdrawn. Some children may act overly cautious (such as refusing to eat safe foods, constantly checking food labels). Some may increase risk-taking behavior (such as eating new foods without checking the ingredients).
- Social Signs: children may seek attention in unhealthy ways, generate conflicts, or withdraw from people and social events.
- Cognitive Signs: obsessive thinking, hyper-vigilance, reduced mental concentration and focus. Children may seem preoccupied or detached, and school performance can suffer.

Ways to Help Your Child Manage Anxiety

- Encourage your child to hold a lovey during a stressful situation.
- Create a 'calm box' with your child that includes items that could help comfort him/her in a stressful situation (e.g. a favorite picture book, a squishy stress relief ball, calming essential oil, a pinwheel).
- Make a glitter jar with your child and encourage him/her to shake it up and then watch the glitter fall to the bottom.
- Teach your child to take deep breaths and practicing mindful breathing (e.g. breathe in to a count of three while focusing on your belly rising, then breathe out for a count of three while focusing on your belly falling).
- Teach your child the lion breath (breathe out with your tongue out and make an audible 'ahhhh' sound), snake breath (make an audible 'sssssssss' sound as you breathe out), bee breath (make an audible 'hmmmmm' sound as you breath out), and bear breath (breath in for a count of four and breathe out for a count of five).
- Introduce mindfulness to your children or strengthen their mindfulness skills. You can find many free online resources by searching for "mindfulness resources for kids." For example, watch Deepak Chopra's 'Guided Meditation for Kids with Deepak Chopra: Teaching Inspiration' on YouTube, or read Dr. Kristen Race's 'Mindful Parenting' book.

- Encourage your child to count to ten slowly.
- Help your child imagine being in a happy place.
- Help your child imagine a positive outcome in an anxiety-provoking situation. Write a story with your child and include imagery of the anxiety-provoking situation and your child overcoming it.
- Teach your child calming yoga poses (e.g. the warrior series, cat-cow, downward facing dog, tree pose, happy baby, child pose, corpse pose/savasana).
- Encourage your child to talk things through with a friend, family member, or trusted adult.
- Practice what to do in a food allergy emergency, including how it would feel to be restrained during the epinephrine injection. Use the epinephrine auto-injector training device with your child.
- Discuss what you can do together to keep your child safe:
  - Read ingredient labels
  - Ask questions about foods
  - Always carry epinephrine
  - Wash hands (with soap or a wet wipe) before eating or touching your face
  - Be aware of your surroundings
  - Bring safe snacks and treats
  - Speak up and tell friends and adults about your food allergy and what to do in an emergency.

- Talk to your allergist about doing a "proximity food challenge" to help ease anxiety. This involves being in the same room as the food allergen at the doctor's office but not actually touching or eating the food.
- Some doctors will perform a 'happy' visit; patients who have been very anxious or had a prior negative experience at the doctor's office can come in for just a discussion or to play in the exam room or waiting room.
- Communicate with the doctor or nurse about the most effective ways of comforting your child during the visit.
- Seek professional help and talk to a psychologist.

Keep in mind that the above techniques should be practiced regularly so they become more engrained behaviors for your child. Parents and caretakers should also acknowledge and find ways to manage their own anxiety about food allergies.

About the Author

Nicole Ondatje has been an advocate for children with food allergies for nearly a decade. She founded S.A.F.E (Supporting Allergic Families through Education) of Boulder County, a community-based organization dedicated to improving the health, safety, and well-being of families with food allergies through increased awareness and education (www.foodallergysafe.org). She has served as a collaborator on an Emergency Medical Services Anaphylaxis Task Force, and as an Allergy & Asthma Network 'Anaphylaxis Community Expert' and trainer. She lives in Colorado with her husband and her daughter who is severely allergic to peanuts and pine nuts.

CPSIA information can be obtained
at www.ICGtesting.com
Printed in the USA
BVHW021109010421
603932BV00004B/154

9 781839 340154